A map!

Written by Charlotte Raby

Illustrated by Dusan Pavlic

Collins

map

pad

3

map

4

pad

tap

dad

· · ·

tap

dad

pit

tip

pit

tip

Review: After reading

Use your assessment from hearing the children read to choose any GPCs and words that need additional practice.

Read 1: Decoding

- Read pages 3, 6, 10 and 11. After each page, ask: Can you point to the letter that makes the /p/ sound?
- Turn to pages 10 and 11, model reading the words with overt blending, then show the children how you can read each word by blending in your head. Ask the children to read the words by trying to blend in their heads.
- Look at the "I spy sounds" pages (14–15) together. Ask the children to point out as many things that they can in the picture that begin with the /m/ sound. (*mole, molehill, magpie, mouse, milk, map, muffin, mushrooms, mangoes*)

Read 2: Vocabulary

- Go back over the three spreads and discuss the pictures. Encourage children to talk about details that stand out for them. Use a dialogic talk model to expand on their ideas and recast them in full sentences as naturally as possible.
- Work together to expand vocabulary by naming objects in the pictures that children do not know.
- Look at page 11 and talk about what 'tip' means. Can children mime tipping something out?

Read 3: Comprehension

- Ask the children:
  - How did the children in the story know where to dig a pit? (*they used a map*)
  - On page 6, what does the boy tap? (*the map*)
- Discuss the picture on pages 14 and 15. Let the children work in pairs to take turns to tap something in the picture for the other to name. Encourage them to ask: What am I tapping?